D0412166

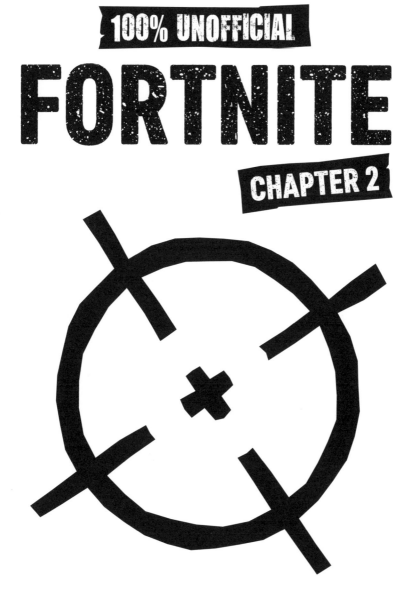

# 100% UNOFFICIAL
# FORTNITE
## CHAPTER 2

# ESSENTIAL GUIDE

This edition published in Great Britain 2020 by Dean,
an imprint of Egmont UK Limited
2 Minster Court, 10th floor, London EC3R 7BB
www.egmont.co.uk

Written by Dan Lipscombe
Edited by Craig Jelley
Designed by Design Button

© Egmont UK Limited 2020

ISBN 978 0 6035 7895 3
71160/001
Printed in Italy

All rights reserved. No part of this publication may be reproduced,
stored in a retrieval system, or transmitted, in any form or by any means,
electronic, mechanical, photocopying, recording or otherwise,
without the prior permission of the publisher and copyright owner.

All in-game images: © 2020 Epic Games, Inc.

**ONLINE SAFETY FOR YOUNGER FANS**

Spending time online is great fun! Here are a few simple rules to help younger
fans stay safe and keep the internet a great place to spend time.
For more advice and guidance, please see page 62 of this book.

- Never give out your real name – don't use it as your username.
- Never give out any of your personal details.
- Never tell anybody which school you go to or how old you are.
- Never tell anybody your password, except a parent or guardian.
- Be aware that you must be 13 or over to create an account on many sites. Always check
the site policy and ask a parent or guardian for permission before registering.
- Always tell a parent or guardian if something is worrying you.

Stay safe online. Any website addresses listed in this book are correct at the
time of going to print. However, Egmont is not responsible for content hosted by
third parties. Please be aware that online content can be subject to change and
websites can contain content that is unsuitable for children. We advise that
all children are supervised when using the internet.

Egmont takes its responsibility to the planet and its inhabitants very seriously.
We aim to use papers from well-managed forests run by responsible suppliers.

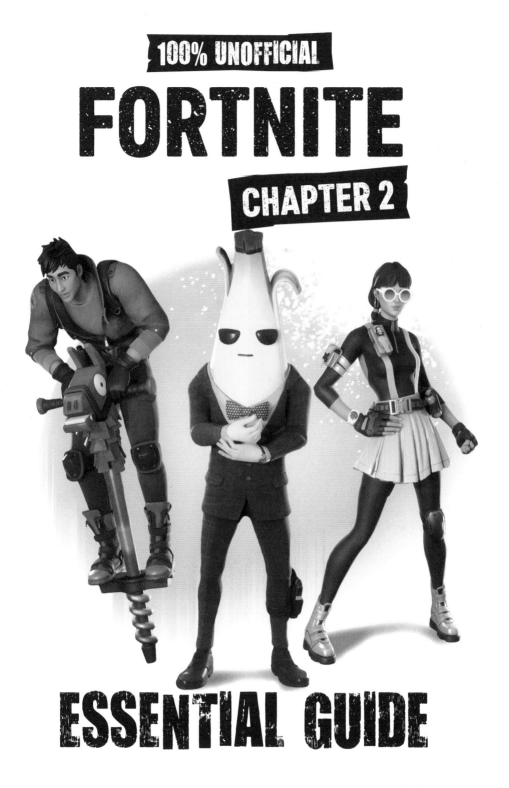

# CONTENTS

# INTRODUCTION

## Were you there when the world collapsed? Millions of players were.

We all went into the end of Season X wondering what would happen. It was another rocket launch, and everyone was busy building platforms to watch it go up. And up it went, right into a rift. Suddenly there were seven rockets all zooming around the sky, in and out of cracks in space.

With no warning, players were blasted backwards, flying through the air just in time to watch the entire map be sucked into a black hole. Players lurking in the lobby saw their character and icons pulled into nothingness. For hours, millions of us sat watching the black hole, not knowing when Fortnite would come back.

For hours we stared at that black hole, until suddenly, a new cutscene welcomed us to a whole new world and a whole new chapter in the life of the most popular Battle Royale on the planet.

Things are very different on this island though. The map has changed, the majority of weapons and items have been vaulted in favour of fishing rods and now we can swim! This is Fortnite Chapter 2 and this is our unofficial guide to what's going on.

Welcome to the new world – let's drop in!

# THE VISITOR

All through Season X of what we're now calling Chapter 1, bubbles appeared over locations across the map. Inside these bubbles, time worked differently – taking players back to the Wild West in Tilted, Celebrating Taco Time at Greasy Grove and even freezing time completely around Loot Lake.

During the season, players were tasked with exploring the map to find tape recordings of someone called 'The Visitor'. Nobody knew who this Visitor was, only that he had been coming to the world of Fortnite for quite some time. Collecting all of the recordings, would allow you to listen to his research ...

... The deciphered message read:

"What the Seven of us are attempting is very risky.
I suspect They are not the only ones watching. But it
must be done or we lose the Bridge forever.

I speculate that no one calculated the formation of the
Island. That interdimensional matter collisions would
resolve rather than push. Now that I witness it first
hand, it's obvious that Pinching alone made
it inevitable.

When I hear this, again, will it help me remember? Or
once Looped will I be just as muted as the others? No
matter – it seems the lengthy precautions worked. The
(unintelligible) Theorem was a success!

I ... us ... you arrived outside the loop at the
exact moment of expansion. This effectively paused
the singularity, giving us time to create the devices
needed to synchronise the Junction.

What I didn't factor was that the only way to trigger
the device was from within the Loop itself. Thus this
hasty and primitive recording.

And why now you ... I find myself Looped. Activate
the beacon at precisely the moment this timer reaches
nothing.

The Zero Point must be contained once more. If They are
correct, it will be the end." >>[000/0000154]>>

# THE END

**The Visitor had predicted The End! It was all there for us to discover, but nobody knew what would happen next. The final days of Season X were upon us and millions of players around the world gathered at Dusty Depot, where a rocket waited to lift off.**

As the timer ticked down, players had their weapons taken away. Health bars vanished and we were left standing on platforms trying to get the best view of a momentous occasion. A rocket took off, cracking through the rift above and spawning seven more rockets that zoomed through the sky, in and out of other rifts.

Suddenly, the rockets grouped together directly above Dusty Depot. The explosive mass congregated around a hanging meteor before falling to the ground and causing a huge explosion centred on the Depot. Nothing survived.

The detonation flung players away from the Depot, before the force sucked everything back to the epicentre. Everything on the map, including players, vehicles and buildings was destroyed and sucked into a black hole.

# THE BLACK HOLE

We all sat around watching the dark void in case something happened. Pulses flashed from within the black hole and numbers began to appear on our screens intermittently, as the community rallied to work out what these mysterious numerals could mean. Luckily it didn't take long for someone to work out ...

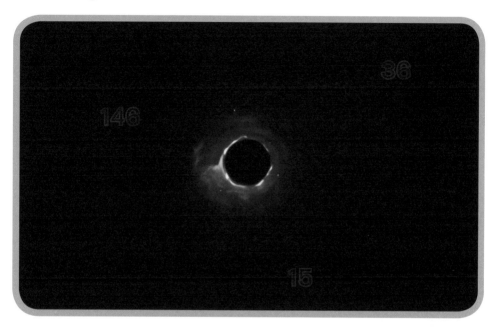

11 - 146 - 15 - 62 - 87 - 14 - 106 - 2 - 150 - 69 - 146 - 15 - 36 - 2 - 176 - 8 - 160 - 65

After some detective work, the code was cracked. The numbers related to words in The Visitor's original recordings. For example, the number 11 meant we needed the eleventh word in the recordings, and so on. The final message read ...

**I WAS NOT ALONE. OTHERS ARE OUTSIDE THE LOOP. THIS WAS NOT CALCULATED. THE ZERO POINT IS NOW INEVITABLE.**

Nobody knew exactly what this meant, but we could assume that we were about to reach a 'zero point'. It turns out that this meant a complete reset of the world we'd grown to know and love. Even though we knew something was coming, we had no idea exactly what was about to happen. Nothing would be the same again.

# CHAPTER 2

Fortnite was 'gone' for almost two days. In that time, we waited, then suddenly, as quickly as it had vanished, it came back.

When the black hole began to subside, we saw an almost-familiar universe in front of us, coloured the traditional Fortnite purple. A foot stepped into view and we saw some new and recognisable faces setting out to explore the new world. From the beginning, we could tell that something was different – many things in fact ...

We were taken on a brief tour of locations across this new island. There were new locations, like a power plant spewing purple goo into the water, new spots for fishing and new mountain ranges that were ripe for exploring (and perfect vantage points for snipers).

As the Battle Bus zoomed into view above the island, the party was bouncing along inside. Our old friend Jonesy leapt out of his seat and through the exit at the back of the bus. As he skydived down towards this new land, we took control, we were going into our first match.

Even the screen was different. Health and shield bars had moved, an experience bar sprawled across the foot of the screen and eliminations, chest searches and simply surviving dished out not only XP, but medals. There was a lot to learn ...

# THE NEW ISLAND

Things changed in past seasons but the new Chapter has brought a brand new island to Fortnite.

## NORTH-WEST

The archipelago of islands to the north-west may seem out of the way, but it's an ideal quiet spot to gather early materials and find a moment of peace before the storm.

## SWEATY SANDS

A relaxing holiday in Fortnite? That will never happen, but Sweaty Sands is a nice coastal spot to visit! With lots of fishing and motorboats, it's an ideal seaside escape.

## SLURPY SWAMP

This is where they make all those lovely Slurps that charge our shields. Unfortunately, the factory is leaking Slurp into the nearby rivers. It's dark and murky, but there's plenty of shield potential.

## SOUTH-EAST

Here you'll find the highest mountain on the new map. It's not much use at the moment, but it certainly gives a lovely view of this new world.

## STEAMY STACKS

This is a great new area to explore and is very similar to the old Pressure Plant. You can even jump into the huge cooling towers and float out of the top to redeploy.

## MORE LOCALES

Keep reading to discover more in-depth details on the new island locations that you'll be waging warfare in.

# NEW LOCATIONS

Although there are a couple of old favourites dotted around the map, the majority of the locations are brand new and ready to explore. Some locations are better than others for early game setup and some are just pure fun with friends. Each one offers something different to visitors, and all of them deserve at least one visit to check them out.

## CRAGGY CLIFFS

The most northerly location on the map offers escape by land and water. It's a smaller area than some others, so enemies can be packed in tight, but you can always hop on a boat to get some breathing room. There are plenty of chances to fish and lots of little hidey-holes where you can take cover if things get too chaotic.

## STEAMY STACKS

Steamy Stacks is always a gamble, but one that can pay off if you're smart. There's plenty of metal to farm and chances for loot are good. However, most buildings are quite open, making you an easy target. The big cooling towers propel you into the sky on a stream of hot air for easy map traversal and there are some cute nods to Chapter 1 in the form of a Kevin statue. If we could guess anything from that opening cutscene of Chapter 2, it would be that Steamy Stacks will be a focus of the action.

# FRENZY FARM

Not so different from Chapter 1's Fatal Fields, Frenzy Farm is a bit more open than the previous agricultural hotspot. There's plenty of wood to harvest from barns and fences, and several buildings are littered with chests and weapons, particularly the main farmhouse. The barns also give a great line of sight for snipers as opponents flee across the open fields.

# SWEATY SANDS

Sweaty Sands has the advantage of being located on the waterfront close to a small cluster of islands. There are plenty of boats and opportunities to go fishing. The central hotel building provides a good view of the surrounding areas so ambushes are unlikely if you're holing up here. It has an abundance of every kind of material, there are lots of hidden chests and if you're lucky enough to commandeer a boat, you can head down the nearby river, which will take you directly to the centre of the map – perfect for when you're facing a fast-moving storm circle.

### RISKY REELS

Okay, so it's not Risky Reels as we know it, but this drive-in cinema, located at the edge of Frenzy Farm, is loaded with loot and materials (those cars give out plenty of metal), and you can climb the cinema screen for easy high-ground too.

# DIRTY DOCKS

The Docks offer so much to players – a huge stock of metal, plenty of high ground and small spaces to hide in. Drop onto the top of the cranes and you'll likely find several chests to get you set up. Of course, it's a long way to run down, but the winding stairs allow cover. From here, you can leap into a motorboat and head around the coast or keep exploring. The storage containers offer lots of little surprises and the nearby hills are the base for power cables which act as zip-lines for quick movement and redeployment.

# HOLLY HEDGES

An area with many similarities to Pleasant Park, this new housing area is a location that offers a bit of everything – materials, chests, hiding places and quick access to weapons. You won't find too much difference between here and other housing areas, but Holly Hedges is beside the Weeping Woods, so you can dart in and out to replenish wood. Unless the storm circle ends up here, it's not a place to hang around, as most of the cover will be harvested or destroyed pretty quickly.

# WEEPING WOODS

So this is where people go camping in Fortnite – and we don't mean laying in wait for enemies. Camper vans and tents are spread throughout the woods, which, when destroyed, often leave behind ammo crates and chests. There's a river nearby, a small lake for fishing, as well as a huge visitor centre that's bursting with materials and loot. With all those trees, there's plenty of wood to collect, but those camper vans will help with metal stocks too. It's a nice place to drop for early cover.

### CENTRE ISLAND

Two weeks into the new Chapter, the mansions that sat within the centre island were knocked down by the Storm King. Who knows what will happen here – from above it looks like a bullseye and who knows, maybe there's still a vault under there …

# LAZY LAKE

Fishing is one of the most important new aspects of Chapter 2 and Lazy Lake is the place to go for a nice spot of angling. Of course, like many of the of the good new fishing spots, you'll be most successful if you're traversing the area by boat, otherwise you'll be left swimming for your life when enemies swarm on you. There are ways to speed up your movement through water, but for someone with a sniper rifle, you will still be an easy target. Toward the edges of the lake, you'll find an industrial area full of factories and habitats that are useful for quick loot.

# SLURPY SWAMP

Nobody likes pollution, but the rivers here flow with Slurp Juice – a couple of minutes wading through these waters will fill your shield! If you don't want to sit in the open water, you can always break the tankers and containers, which will splash you with Slurp instead. There's not too much loot here, but nearby houses have an acceptable amount, as well as some movement cover. Slurpy Swamp is perhaps the most unique place on the new map – it has a murky aesthetic that stands out from the bright landscapes beyond.

# MISTY MEADOWS

You can find Misty Meadows towards the south of the map. It offers a mixture of housing, tourist buildings and fishing spots. It's a pretty harbour town (at least before the shooting starts) with access available via boat. Misty is split in two by a river, which offers some tactical opportunities as people move from one side to the other across the bridge! If the fighting gets too hectic or you need to escape, you'll find two mountains in close proximity offering high-ground and a couple of surprises.

### E.G.O. OUTPOSTS

Spread out across the map, these army style encampments are often loaded with loot and materials. Just be careful you don't try to harvest the new explosive barrels or you're going to have a very bad day.

# NEW SCREEN LAYOUT

You might have noticed that there are some changes and additions to the screen you've become so familiar with. We'll delve into some of the big updates later on, but for now let's look at some of the obvious changes.

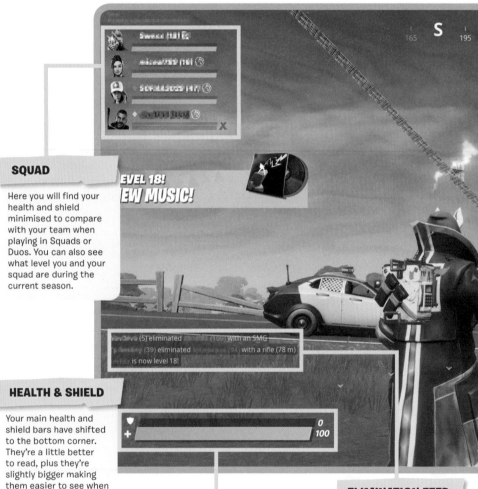

## SQUAD

Here you will find your health and shield minimised to compare with your team when playing in Squads or Duos. You can also see what level you and your squad are during the current season.

## HEALTH & SHIELD

Your main health and shield bars have shifted to the bottom corner. They're a little better to read, plus they're slightly bigger making them easier to see when you're in the middle of a fight.

## ELIMINATION FEED

This list will be populated with all the major events that happen during a match, including eliminations and levelling.

## MINI-MAP

The mini-map hasn't really changed that much, except now when you're skydiving you'll notice there's a bar on the left that shows you how close to the ground you are. It's a nice addition to help judge your landing spot.

## MATCH INFO

This section will show you how many kills you've made, the number of remaining players, as well as the progress towards your objective if you're playing an LTM.

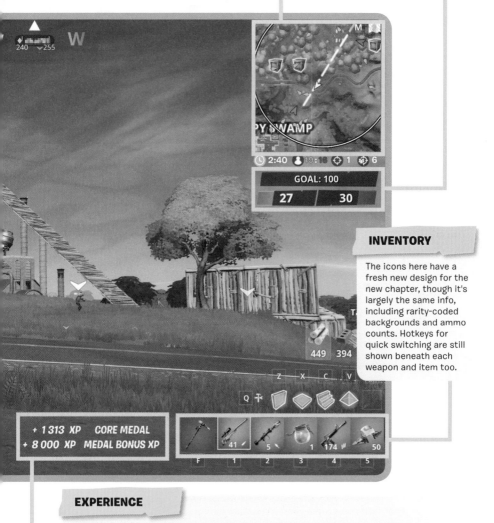

## INVENTORY

The icons here have a fresh new design for the new chapter, though it's largely the same info, including rarity-coded backgrounds and ammo counts. Hotkeys for quick switching are still shown beneath each weapon and item too.

## EXPERIENCE

Experience is a much bigger focus of Fortnite in Chapter 2. Everything you do rewards an amount of XP – from opening ammo crates to eliminating enemies. This section of the screen will show you exactly how much XP you're earning from each action. If you level up during a match, you'll see that the reward you have just unlocked flashes up on the screen beneath the squad list.

# THE BATTLE PASS

A huge part of the Fortnite experience is the Battle Pass and thankfully, it hasn't changed much for Chapter 2. There are still 100 levels, the Pass still dishes out emotes, stickers, skins, gliders and contrails. However, Epic has made a few quality-of-life tweaks to make it easier to see which rewards you've earned, and which are available in the not-too-distant future.

CHAPTER 2

## SEASON 2

GIFT BATTLE PASS

REPLAY VIDEO

SHADOW

VIEW CHOICE

### RARITY

Unlockables are underlined with a colour representing their rarity, easily highlighting how rare your next reward is.

### PROGRESS

You'll notice that all of the items available on the Battle Pass are now displayed across the bottom of the screen. This allows for much easier viewing of what the item is and what it does. It's much clearer to see which level you need to reach to unlock that desired skin or emote.

31  32  33 FREE!  35

is not eligible for refund.
ason 2 through April 30th.

PAGE 4 OF 10

As well as seeing what you've unlocked during a match, you'll still be able to properly explore each newly available item when you return to the lobby, including the option to equip!

## ITEM INFO

This section details everything you need to know about the selected reward, including the type, rarity, name and link to more info.

BONUS : TOON BLAST! Unleash TNTina's toon form with Boom!, **THE FIRST CEL-SHADED TRANSFORMATION EMOTE.**

## COLOUR CHANGE

Skins that come in different colour varieties or styles will scroll through the options if highlight the skin tile at the bottom of the screen. In Season 2, you can choose a faction that affects some of the skins you unlock

# MEDALS AND XP

So players can earn XP faster, the devs have created a 'punchcard' that slowly fills up with medals as you play and complete certain achievements. The card refreshes each day encouraging you to sign in and earn more medals. It can all be a bit confusing though, so we've broken down which medals you can earn, how to earn them and how much XP they give.

You'll find an empty punchcard on the main menu each day. As you play, achieving milestones will reward you with a medal, which can be upgraded as you repeat your achievements. Each medal has three levels – Bronze, Silver and Gold – that will bestow you with increasing XP. Take a look at some medals you can get your hands on.

### FIRST MATCH
The easiest medal to achieve is this one, which simply requires you to join and play a single match.

### SCAVENGER
Loot chests, supply drops or Llamas. Search 3 of these items for Bronze, 7 for Silver and 10 for Gold.

### BATTLE
Eliminate opponents to advance the Battle medal. 1 will get you Bronze, 4 will get Silver and 8 will land you Gold.

### SURVIVOR
Reach the top 50 of a match to get the Bronze Survivor medal, the top 25 for Silver and the top 10 for Gold.

### SNIPER
You need to hit a long-distance shot of at least 100 metres to land the sniper medal. Better get some practice in!

### FISHING
Catch something with a fishing rod to reel in the fishing medal – it doesn't even have to be a fish ...

**MEDAL PUNCHCARD**

Every medal you earn will reward you with an amount of XP. The first four medals of the day give 8k XP each, with the fifth medal rewarding 16k XP. The following four switch back to 8k each, before the tenth medal gives you a final boost of 16k XP.

If you're playing well, you could easily fill your punchcard in a few matches. Choosing a game mode with respawns, such as Team Rumble, will help you achieve goals quicker – it gives you longer to loot and more eliminations.

SCORE MEDAL
Reached Team Score 50

+ 1,313 XP  SCORE MEDAL
+ 8,000 XP  MEDAL BONUS XP

**TOP TIP**
Loot everything you possibly can and fish often. XP is given for pretty much every action in Fortnite now, so stay active and earn points.

# EXPERIENCE POINTS (XP)

XP isn't just earned through medals. Simple actions like opening an ammo crate or chomping a mushroom will also reward you with XP. It all totals up quite naturally, but below we've listed some of the most common ways to earn big numbers.

 **ELIMINATIONS –** Your first elimination will reward you with 50XP earning an extra 20XP for each elim after that.

 **PLACEMENT –** A Victory Royale will give you 300XP, coming second rewards 200XP. Between 3rd and 10th nets 100XP and 11th – 20th place gives you 25XP.

 **SURVIVAL TIME –** This is how many storm phases you survive. With the lowest being 17XP for the first phase, through to 238XP for getting to the final circle.

# SWIMMING

The new map has brought a lot of water with it. There are more rivers, lakes and beaches than before, but you can't always rely on the much sought-after motorboats. Often your only way to move is to swim. No more jumping and walking through waist-high water, now there are depths for you to dive into!

Swimming through water is now faster than walking through it, which gives you a whole new way to travel around the map. Just dive in and move in the direction you want to go to automatically start swimming.

However, you can swim even faster with some well-timed button presses. Jumping will see you break the surface of the water like a dolphin, diving back under the waves.

As you do this, you'll see a visible burst of speed. By jumping at the right point – the end of the boost – you'll move much faster through the water.

Swimming isn't all gentle dips in the water – for one, it'll make you a sitting duck for snipers. When you burst from the water, a well-timed shot will break your rhythm and cause you to take more damage. Damage from shots is lessened while you're underwater though.

## WATER RESISTANCE

Fortunately, to provide some extra defensive cover, you can still build. It takes some skilful movement and timing, but it's entirely possible to build yourself some nice overhead cover to protect from shots while you plan your next move.

# FISHING

Releasing a map with so much water opened up lots of options, but the most important is fishing. It's not just a little bit of fun for you and your friends – though it's definitely enjoyable – using fishing rods can land you important items for the match. So grab a pole and find a good spot to cast your line.

## FIND YOUR FISHING ROD

Fishing rods can be found pretty much anywhere on the map but are most frequently found near water. They'll appear in chests or can be seen sticking out of barrels which, when broken, drop two or three at a time.

## HOW TO FISH

Fishing is very easy in Fortnite. Just equip your rod and as you hold down the 'shoot' button, you'll see a light blue arc in the air with a target circle on the end. That circle tells you where the line will land, which is helpful for targeting hot spots. When you have something on your line, you'll see a small splash on the surface and hear the ripple of the water. As soon as you spot this, tap the button again and you'll pull your catch ashore.

# WHERE TO FISH

You can fish pretty much anywhere you want. Where there's water, there's a chance to catch something. It can be a lake, river or along the coast. But fishing into any old patch of water won't land you a big catch. Fishing in a regular spot will usually end with ammo, materials or smaller fish which do very little healing. You may even find an old tin can which is pretty useless in a fight.

Find areas where the water splashes and creates white rings on the surface. This is a 'hot spot', which is where the best catches are. Fishing here can net you everything from rare weapons to super fish that do massive damage to enemies. Weapon drops are random, as with chests, but you'll never hook a common or uncommon weapon from a hot spot.

# CATCH OF THE DAY

What lurks beneath the calm blue waters? As well as a seemingly endless supply of discarded weapons and items, there are now a host of fishy friends that can aid you in battle. Sort of anyway, their fins are too small for them to be squadmates ...

## SMALL FRY (COMMON)

Small Fry generally act like bandages, healing for 25pts per fish, up to the 75 health mark. At this point you can't eat anymore. They're great in a tight spot, but should be dropped in favour of something better.

## FLOPPER (UNCOMMON)

A Flopper gives you 50pts of health. This is probably the best healing item in the game currently. All fish take only a second to eat, compared to 10 seconds for a med-kit. Chomping two of these takes much less time and gets you back to full health.

**TOP TIP**
Go fishing early in the game when there are fewer people around you. Stock up on Floppers for those quick and easy heals.

## SLURPFISH (EPIC)

Slurpfish act like the old Chug Splash, healing you just where you need it. If you're at full health, eating one of these will give you 50pts of shield. If you're very low on health, it will focus on healing 50pts to health. The best thing about a Slurpfish is that it can split these 50 points; if you're on 75 health with no shield, you'll receive a full heal and 25pts of shield.

## MYTHIC GOLDFISH (LEGENDARY)

The rarest fish of them all. So rare that only a few have been found so far in millions of matches. There's no use eating this one as it's in fact a throwable weapon. It will deal 90pts of damage if you land a direct hit on an opponent, otherwise it'll flop away without any effect.

## FISHING TIPS:

- You can move while fishing. Just as you would when harvesting. Make sure you're not standing still while at the water – you become an easy target.

- You can also fish through windows of bases if you prefer. This will give you some protection, but isn't the stealthiest of hideouts ...

- It's possible to fish loot from the floor with a fishing rod. After a fight, if you see a precious gun, simply snag it with your rod.

- And it's not just weapons. You can even yank enemies or a downed teammate towards you! Very helpful for taking people by surprise or bringing a friend to safety for a revival.

**TOP TIP**
The Harpoon Gun acts like a much faster fishing rod, but has limited uses. It can also break wooden builds in one shot, or pull an enemy towards you at speed.

31

# GAME CHANGERS

There are some things that, when added to the game, take everything we know about the way we play Fortnite and turn it on its head. These epic updates come in many forms and we're going to look at a couple of the biggest that were released along with Chapter 2!

## HIDING

The ability to hide in Chapter 1 was limited to finding a bush item and running around in a silly disguise. Those piles of hay and dumpsters used to mean nothing more than a handful of wood or metal when harvested, but now they have a whole new purpose.

Look out for open dumpsters or piles of hay and when you approach them, you'll be given the option to hide. Be aware though, when hiding, you can't reload or swap weapons. If you plan on leaping out and surprising someone, prepare before hiding.

**TOP TIP**
Dumpsters and hay bales can be harvested, so you can remove them from the area quickly to stop others from hiding.

The bushes you'll find in open grassy areas now give you the option of hiding too. Once you stand in the middle, nobody will be able to see you. There's no button to hide, simply walk in. However, they don't stop others from wandering in and finding you.

# MOTORBOAT

The Motorboat is a wonky but lovable beast on the water. Controlled in a very different way to previous vehicles, it holds all four members of a squad, has a short boost available and fires rockets from the front. Your team can choose between firing shots at enemy squads or casting off to do some fishing.

A fresh Motorboat starts with 800 hit points, meaning it can take a fair bit of damage before you need to abandon ship. It is quite a big target, so even assault rifles and pistols can take good shots at it. Unlike older vehicles, you don't have a great deal of protection while driving. It's entirely possible for a good sniper to eliminate you while you're speeding past.

The rockets are a good damage dealer (35 points per rocket) but aren't particularly accurate. It's great to use the boat's weapons to weaken structures or lay down covering fire before hopping out for a proper firefight.

# WEAPONS AND ITEMS

Chapter 2 could be seen as a full reset of the game and that is most noticeable in the weapon and item loot available. Gone are the Chug Jugs, Quad Rocket Launchers and Heavy Snipers; now we have a basic roster of items. Of course, they still come in the usual rarities, but there is a lot less choice now compared to Chapter One. The same rule applies as before, the higher the rarity, the better the weapon generally.

## WEAPONS

### ASSAULT RIFLE

The Assault Rifle is great for laying down a constant spray of shots. It lacks accuracy because the gun has significant recoil when it fires, but it will take down opponents and structures equally well. It's a great mid-range weapon but can also be used up close if you can keep an enemy in the crosshairs.

| | |
|---|---|
| DAMAGE | ☐☐☐☐☐ |
| FIRE RATE | ☐☐☐☐☐ |
| MAG SIZE | ☐☐☐☐☐ |
| RELOAD | ☐☐☐☐☐ |

### BURST ASSAULT RIFLE

While the Burst Assault Rifle does slightly less damage than the standard Assault Rifle, it's much easier to control because it fires short flurries of bullets. This makes it a lot more accurate and gives you the chance to use it at a distance, because the gun has a narrower spray in short bursts.

| | |
|---|---|
| DAMAGE | ☐☐☐☐☐ |
| FIRE RATE | ☐☐☐☐☐ |
| MAG SIZE | ☐☐☐☐☐ |
| RELOAD | ☐☐☐☐☐ |

# SMG

The SMG is best used at close-range, to barrage your enemy with bullets, or to help with breaking down structures. Because of how fast the SMG fires its shots, it does more damage than Rifles or Pistols. It becomes less effective at a distance

DAMAGE ☐☐☐☐☐
FIRE RATE ☐☐☐☐☐
MAG SIZE ☐☐☐☐☐
RELOAD ☐☐☐☐☐

# PISTOL

Nobody expects the pistol to be an effective weapon. It's small and usually not very powerful, however, it fires as fast as you can hit the trigger, plus it has a quick reload time. It can also be dangerous from a distance with practice and patience.

DAMAGE ☐☐☐☐☐
FIRE RATE ☐☐☐☐☐
MAG SIZE ☐☐☐☐☐
RELOAD ☐☐☐☐☐

**EVERY** weapon is available in every rarity. Unlike the previous chapter, when some weapons would have rarer versions and others wouldn't, all guns in Chapter 2 are equal.

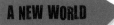
# WEAPONS

## PUMP SHOTGUN

The Pump has a slightly higher damage rate than its Tactical sibling, but has an inferior fire rate, meaning it is a little bit slower. It packs a punch from short range and can easily cut down an enemy with one or two shots, even through a full shield.

| DAMAGE | ☐☐☐☐☐ |
| FIRE RATE | ☐☐☐☐ |
| MAG SIZE | ☐☐☐☐☐ |
| RELOAD | ☐☐☐☐☐ |

## TACTICAL SHOTGUN

While it's slightly less powerful than the Pump, many pro players prefer the speedy Tactical Shotgun because of its tight bullet spread. This means more of the bullets are likely to hit the target and cause more damage to an enemy overall.

| DAMAGE | ☐☐☐☐☐ |
| FIRE RATE | ☐☐☐☐☐ |
| MAG SIZE | ☐☐☐☐☐ |
| RELOAD | ☐☐☐☐☐ |

# ROCKET LAUNCHER

The main idea behind the Rocket Launcher is carnage. It's best used sparingly to destroy builds, as it takes ages to reload. Make sure to switch to a pistol or AR while you're waiting. It's quite hard to hit a moving target with a rocket as well ...

| | | | | | |
|---|---|---|---|---|---|
| **DAMAGE** | ☐ | ☐ | ☐ | ☐ | ☐ |
| **FIRE RATE** | ☐ | ☐ | ☐ | ☐ | ☐ |
| **MAG SIZE** | ☐ | ☐ | ☐ | ☐ | ☐ |
| **RELOAD** | ☐ | ☐ | ☐ | ☐ | ☐ |

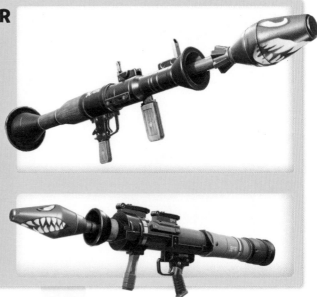

# BOLT-ACTION SNIPER

The only sniper to survive the cull is the Bolt-Action. These rifles pack a punch and are designed for long-range encounters. The reload rates between shots is huge at the lower rarities so make sure to upgrade to epic and beyond – you'll notice the difference.

| | | | | | |
|---|---|---|---|---|---|
| **DAMAGE** | ☐ | ☐ | ☐ | ☐ | ☐ |
| **FIRE RATE** | ☐ | ☐ | ☐ | ☐ | ☐ |
| **MAG SIZE** | ☐ | ☐ | ☐ | ☐ | ☐ |
| **RELOAD** | ☐ | ☐ | ☐ | ☐ | ☐ |

# HEALING AND SHIELDS

## BANDAGES

**TIME TO USE:** 4 seconds

**TOTAL BENEFIT:** 25 health points

**MAX STACK:** 15

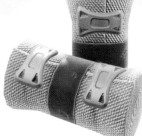

## MED-KIT

**TIME TO USE:** 10 seconds

**TOTAL BENEFIT:** 100 health points

**MAX STACK:** 3

## MINI SHIELD

**TIME TO USE:** 4 seconds

**TOTAL BENEFIT:** 25 shield points

**MAX STACK:** 6

## SHIELD POTION

**TIME TO USE:** 5 seconds

**TOTAL BENEFIT:** 50 shield points

**MAX STACK:** 3

## BANDAGE BAZOOKA

**TIME TO USE:** as long as it takes to shoot a friend!

**TOTAL BENEFIT:** 15 health points per shot. Recharges every 20 seconds and takes up TWO inventory slots!

# FISH

The addition of fish introduced a quicker, more appealing alternative to traditional healing items, but they can take a while to get your hands on because you have to fish for them!

## SMALL FRY

**TIME TO USE:** 1 seconds

**TOTAL BENEFIT:** 25 health points

**MAX STACK:** 6

## FLOPPER

**TIME TO USE:** 1 seconds

**TOTAL BENEFIT:** 50 health points

**MAX STACK:** 3

## SLURPFISH

**TIME TO USE:** 1 seconds

**TOTAL BENEFIT:** 50 effective health/shield points

**MAX STACK:** 2

# ITEMS

## MUSHROOM

## APPLE

*Found in woods and around Slurpy Swamp*

**TIME TO USE:** 1 seconds

**TOTAL BENEFIT:** 5 shield points

*Found in woods and shops*

**TIME TO USE:** 1 seconds

**TOTAL BENEFIT:** 5 health points

## GRENADE

The grenade has survived mostly unchanged – it deals 100 damage to players, 375 damage to structures and can be carried in a stack of up to 15.

## FISHING ROD

The humble rod is used for catching fish, ammo and weapons in any body of water.

## HARPOON

Used in a similar way to the fishing rod, but can also damage structures and pull players. Has 10 uses before it breaks apart.

## DAMAGE TRAP

The only trap left in the game is the spike trap. It can be placed on walls, floors and ceilings and causes 150 points of damage to players.

# UPGRADE STATIONS

Epic and Legendary weapons are the best in the game – finding one takes a lot of luck or alternatively, a lot of materials. Upgrade Stations are now dotted around the map in barns, scrapyards and garages. These give you the opportunity to advance your weapon up the rarity tiers.

The stations will demand stacks of materials to increase the rarity level of your currently equipped weapon. For example, using materials to upgrade a rare weapon will change it into an epic weapon, increasing the damage, reload speed and accuracy. They could be compared to the vending machines from Chapter 1, however, the Upgrade Stations don't disappear once used.

For Chapter 2, Fortnite became about balance. Yes, an Upgrade Station could turn your common shotgun to a legendary blaster, but it will take a lot of materials. Do you spend time farming materials so you can guarantee a good weapon, or take your chances on finding one, reserving your materials for build battles? Remember, a healthy stack of materials is as important as a good gun in Fortnite.

# HOW MANY MATERIALS?

The amount of materials that you need to upgrade your gun will depend on the rarity of the weapon. Each upgrade you do will require wood, metal and stone, but in different quantities depending on rarity. Consult this handy chart to find out exactly how many you need of each.

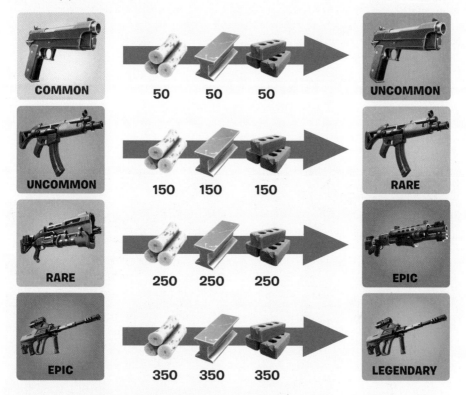

| COMMON | 50 | 50 | 50 | UNCOMMON |
| UNCOMMON | 150 | 150 | 150 | RARE |
| RARE | 250 | 250 | 250 | EPIC |
| EPIC | 350 | 350 | 350 | LEGENDARY |

Remember, not all materials need to be harvested. Many can be found laying out in the open or will be dropped when a player is eliminated. Keep your eyes peeled for piles in the open as they could be just what you need.

# DEFENCE

Defending your position can be as important as aggressively attacking in Fortnite. The situation you find yourself in will always dictate where your focus will lie. Being defensive isn't a bad thing and doesn't always mean 'turtling up' and laying in wait for other players. You can still defend while moving or by creating diversions and hiding in plain sight.

## DEFENSIVE MOVEMENT

Staying safe while moving across the map isn't just moving in odd patterns or jumping a lot. You can build to stay safe too. No matter what situation you find yourself in, there's always a way to build yourself out of trouble.

## FLANKED?

If there's someone to the side of you, placing walls as you run for cover is the easiest way to stop shots hitting you. Wood is fine as it builds quickly but we prefer the safety of brick as it has a better balance between speed and sturdiness. Simply swing your aim to the side of you and place walls as you run!

## PLAYER ABOVE?

If you find yourself on the ground while someone is firing down at you from an elevated position, you can bunker down in a metal 1x1, but this will often mean you're pinned down, which would be especially bad if the storm is closing in. Your best bet is to place a wall or ramp and then add floors above your head to block shots.

# PLAYER BELOW?

High ground is a benefit but doesn't always mean you'll be in the best position. Someone on the ground with an SMG can chew through your builds with speed. So, you'll need to use layers, like a floor with a pyramid on top. This means they have to use more ammo to shred your builds and get a shot at you as you run along above them.

# NATURAL DEFENCES

You don't always have to rely on building for cover. The world is populated with natural cover that you can use in a firefight or as hiding places to sneak around an area. Just be wary that most of it can be shot to pieces!

# PRACTISE!

You don't have to dive straight into competitive matches to get familiar with the mechanics of Fortnite. Sometimes it's a good idea to hop into Creative or Playground with a bunch of friends to practise your skills. By the time you do get into Squads or Duos, you'll be a pro. Here's a few drills you can run!

## HIDE-AND-SEEK

Nothing beats a good game of hide-and-seek to sharpen your enemy-spotting skills – it can also help you to familiarise yourself with all the nooks and crannies that you or your enemies can use across the map. Begin by having your squad drop in the same spot and start a countdown of 60 seconds, in which hiders must find a good spot to lay low. Building to hide yourself is cheating though!

## TAG

Another Fortnite twist on a playground classic is tag! This game is best played in the built-up areas and building is allowed. One person starts as the tagger and has to 'tag' the others by hitting them with their pickaxe and making them the tagger. It's a great way to sharpen your close-combat and dodging skills, as well as brushing up on your building abilities.

# BIG BUILDS

Why not just have a good old-fashioned build-off? You can aim to create a certain structure, or just see who can build the highest. You should be able to practise using the different types of build materials, and if you add in a couple of guns then you can try out some edits to add windows, doors and other helpful structures. Once you drop back into Battle Royale, you'll be a building pro.

# BASES

There will always be a time during the game when you'll need a base, whether you need to heal up safely, or just want to wait out the storm from a good vantage point. Whatever the reason, you need to choose the right base for the right situation. Each of our examples can be built with any material and quick-edited for ease of movement.

## 1X1

A quick 1x1 is the simplest build to hide in. It can be used as a temporary stop to heal or top up shields before jumping back into the fight, or to shield you as you hoover up loot from a kill. If you want to hole up in one for longer, you can add a ramp up one side, which will allow you to pop up, take a shot, then hide again.

## RECTANGLE RAMPS

Build a rectangle measuring 2x1, then add two ramps pointing up from the middle. This is perfect for Duos or Squads as it allows you to hold a position by peeking up and watching different directions.

It's quick to build and can be stacked higher and higher in the same configuration to give you identical cover at a higher vantage point. You could even combine two rectangles into an x-shape (with an additional space in the middle) to allow a vantage for all squad members.

**TOP TIP**
With any base, the higher you can build it, the better it will be. Players will struggle to shoot up, whereas you can fire down with ease.

# RECYCLED BUILDING

There is a way to make an awesome base without using as many materials – modify the existing buildings! Why use precious stone when you already have a brick and mortar house to hide in? You can demolish windows and replace them with solid walls, add sniper towers that peek out the top of the roof and add traps to entrances to prevent invasions from jealous enemy players. Of course, make sure you convert a building that's safely in the storm circle as it will take you a fairly long time to create a base.

# THE CASTLE

If you're overflowing with materials or just can't find an existing building to turn into a fortress, why not create a huge multi-room castle structure filled with boxes, traps, ramps and pyramids?

It's probably a good idea to attempt a build of this magnitude with a squad, as many hands will make light work, and you can edit each other's placed structures. Keep the interior random and maze-like so infiltrators can't surprise you.

# SMART BUILDING

It doesn't matter how accurate you are with an assault rifle, if you can't build well, your win-rate will plummet. Building is essential to Fortnite – it's as important as hitting long-distance snipes or spamming rockets at a base. Practice is the only way to get better at building, so practise these common techniques a lot, even if it's in Creative.

## RAMP-RUSH

It's open ground. Your opponent is in front of you and, unless they're a bot, they're going to try to build around you. The simplest way to counter is by 'ramp-rushing' - building consecutive ramps in order to get the high-ground. The best ramp-rushers will place walls in front of their ramps to protect the structure and prevent fall damage. Wood is a faster, weaker material to build with, but stone and metal will provide more protection. In a build-off situation, usually the person who gets to the high-ground first will win if they can land a couple of shotgun shots.

**TOP TIP**
Use double ramps, which allow you to move side-to-side.

# SNIPER TOWERS

Stacking 1x1s on top of each other will give you a resource-cheap tower that you can turn into an excellent vantage point. You'll be able to see the lie of the land around you and take shots at anyone you see with a sniper rifle.

**TOP TIP**
If you don't have a sniper rifle, don't worry. A good position and an Epic or better AR will do the job just as well.

You have to remember to cover your back and protect yourself from shotgun drops. To do this, place walls on three sides of your tower and a half floor as a roof. You can also use quick edits to drop in a window, offering even less space for your opponent to shoot through.

Sniper towers are a risky strategy because a well-placed rocket could bring your beautiful creation crashing down around you. Build a few towers close together to make it harder for your opponents to spot you.

# ADVANCED SMART BUILDING

As you get more confident with building, especially in high-pressure shootouts, you'll be ready to attempt more daring or time-consuming builds. The builds on these pages are for pro players who have an abundance of bravery and materials. Of course, you can still practise these advanced methods in Creative mode!

## THE MAZE

Perhaps the hardest thing to do in Fortnite is build complex structures while keeping track of where you and your enemy are. If you're being chased through builds, the best thing to do is to start building randomly, forcing your opponent to break down walls to get to you. This either wastes their ammo or their time.

But you can also do this offensively too, by laying down lots of walls, floors and pyramids to confuse them. In order to achieve this, you'll need to master quick edits because if you walk back over your own structures, a quick edit will allow better movement.

Remember, when you first place a structure, it is see-through until fully finished. Use this to predict where your enemy will move to.

If you're feeling confident, you can drop to the ground and tunnel under the confusing maze you built above. Then simply ramp up and above the other player for an easier chance at a shot.

**TOP TIP**
Mix up the materials you place. This will further frustrate the other player.

# DAREDEVIL TURN-AROUND

This move takes guts and quick fingers too. The trick to a good turn-around is to leap off a structure or cliff-face and drop down, placing a ramp beneath you to break your fall. It's the perfect way to escape a vertical battle if you find yourself outnumbered or outmatched. There's no shame in a smart retreat.

The Turn-Around is also a handy trick for stealing the high-ground by ramping around the outside of an opponent's build. If you aim your jump to stick close to the structure, you can place floors or ramps to change your tactics.

Be careful that your enemies don't follow your escape. Or, plan for them to do so and lie in wait to spring a trap.

# EDITING

Fast editing is perhaps the hardest skill to get right in Fortnite. It's the difference between a win and a loss. Before you start practising or using quick edits in games, you need to prepare yourself to miss chances. You're bound to make mistakes, or bound to edit the wrong piece, leading to your elimination. Don't be disheartened, it takes time to develop muscle memory.

## CHANGE YOUR BINDINGS AND SENSITIVITY

So many players neglect their settings! Creative mode isn't just for fun – it's a great place to mess around with new bindings and settings in safety. Head into the Options and adapt the sensitivity settings of your mouse or thumbsticks. Once you get your settings just right, it could mean faster building and faster edits. The same goes for keybindings – you can change the function of any button you want to suit your habits.

## GIVE ME YOUR WALL

The idea of stealing a wall is to replace an enemy's structure with one of your own. You can then edit the piece, allowing access to the hidden opponent. Hit or shoot the wall until it breaks – your opponent will be preparing to replace the wall, but if you're fast, you can place one first. Then it's a case of switching the wall panel for a window, half-wall or diagonal before switching to a weapon and going in for the kill.

# 50% OFF RAMPS!

Ramps are a 'go-to' build for players. They're the basic building component to travel vertically or outbuild opponents in search of high ground. Using the half-ramp, which splits a ramp along its length, is a quick switch which will fool any player chasing you upwards. The ramp needs to be one of your own so that as you reach the top, you turn quickly and edit the ramp into a half-ramp. It will force your opponent to react and move to the correct side of the ramp, and gives you a smaller target to aim at.

**TOP TIP**
Each of these edits require you to be able to switch to your shotgun quickly. Any fight in these situations will be close combat.

# WINDOW SWITCHEROO

This is another edit tactic that relies on reaction speed, though you won't be under pressure from an enemy. The basic premise is to constantly edit between windows and normal walls – you'll have better defence when it's a wall, but be able to shoot freely at opponents when it's a window. The window allows a much smaller target for your enemy to hit, but you'll need to get used to switching between builds, edits and switching to the weapons you want to use.

# PRACTISE MAKES PERFECT

You don't need to have an opponent to practise your edits – just materials and space. Practise alternating between different structures like changing a wall to a window, or cycling between build and edit modes. Once you've mastered these rotations, try to work on switching weapons in between each one. Pull your friends into creative and see which one of you is the fastest.

**TOP TIP**
Don't forget you can sprinkle in a few traps!

# COMMS

Communication is always key to being a team player. Becoming a great team requires more than just enemy position call-outs and weapon drop mentions. We thought it might be a good idea to take a look at some of the terms used by streamers and video creators, while giving a few helpful tips for you and your friends. Master these and your squad will be a force to be reckoned with.

## CALL OUT DAMAGE

If your team is approaching an enemy, it's likely you'll try a few lucky shots from far away. If any of them land, mention the numbers that pop from the player you hit. If they're blue, they still have a shield. If they're white, the shield is down, and you can work out how close they are to being knocked down.

### EXAMPLE:

"Hit them for 45 white" – This will mean they've taken 45 points of damage without a shield. We know that everyone has 100 hit points before being knocked, so this tells your team that the enemy likely has just over half their life bar left.

## PING IT

Season 8 of Chapter 1 brought in a Ping system, which can often be a lifesaver for those with or without a microphone. For console players, the Ping button can be found on the left D-Pad, and on PC it defaults to the middle mouse button, but of course, these can be changed.

The Ping is clever as it knows what you're flagging to your team. If your crosshair is over an item or weapon, it will show an item or weapon icon. If you're hovering over an enemy, the Ping will take the form of a danger symbol. You can even use it to place a waypoint by aiming into the distance and tapping the Ping.

# SHARE RESPONSIBILITY

With a small inventory, there's only so much you can carry on your person. You will want to share certain responsibilities with your team, such as who can hold healing items and who needs the fishing rod. You can't carry all the healing items, so share them out and remind people what you're holding. There's no use in you all carrying similar items, because as you near the end of the game, you'll naturally be closer together so can easily drop what others may need.

## EXAMPLE:

**"I've got 3 minis, can carry more" – This tells your team that if anyone finds minis, you could hold them until they're needed. This means in a squad of four, the other three players can hold other healing items instead.**

**TOP TIP**
Don't forget to ask if you need some healing or ammo. You don't want to be knocked when your teammate had a stack of bandages

# COMM TERMS

**CRACKED –** There's a lovely little cracking sound when you take away someone's shield, usually shown by a falling blue number too. For example, "Cracked their shield!" tells your team that the enemy has no shield and will take fewer hits to eliminate.

**KNOCKED –** Short for 'knocked down', meaning you're health has been depleted and you're stuck in crawling mode and unable to shoot until a team-mate revives you.

**LASERED –** Similar to 'Cracking' someone, dealing a lot of damage in one shot, or a spray from an SMG, you'll hear a laser noise. This is a good thing to point out as it often means one more shot will finish them off.

**ROTATION –** Rotating is what happens at the end of a storm movement, as you're preparing to move into a new safe circle. This is time to check ammo, make sure you have shields and plan your route to the new area.

**TURTLING –** This is a fancy term for camping, really. But turtling means staying in one place, surrounded by metal. This can be a helpful tactic if you're lucky enough to be in the safe circle on each rotation.

**WHITE/BLUE –** This relates to the numbers which pop from enemies when they take damage. If the number is blue they still have shield, unless 'cracked'. If the number is white, then they have no shield at all and can be eliminated quickly.

# LEARN AND ADAPT

There's always something new to learn in Fortnite because of the constant updates. You can be one of the best players in the world and still make mistakes. Remember, it's not about winning or losing, but winning or learning. Here are some common mistakes that we've encountered so you can try to avoid them.

## KEEP THE SAME INVENTORY

That doesn't mean stick to the same weapons and items. Just make sure that you keep them in the same spots on the inventory bar. It only takes a few games to know that your pickaxe never moves from the first slot, but train yourself to keep your main weapon, shotgun, healing item, etc. in the same slots. Selecting them will become second nature.

## DON'T BE TOO DEFENSIVE

Battles are often won by rushing your enemy when they assume you won't. You can't win games by holing up in a box! Watch for an opening – enemies are vulnerable when they're building, reloading or collecting loot. Alternatively, create an opening. Breaking momentum and switching direction while building will cause your enemy to pause while they work out what you're doing. Attacking is about overwhelming your opponent and forcing them to make a mistake.

# KNOW WHEN TO STOP LOOTING

There are players who spend far too long looking for the perfect loadout. Spending too much time hunting chests might be a waste of time if the loot is bad – the contents of chests and weapons on the floor are completely random. Sometimes having a bad weapon and being ready to use it is better than having a great weapon and not being ready. Cut your losses and get out there, you might hit the right shot and be able to take those rare guns from the loot pile.

# TAKE YOUR TIME

Fights are rarely instantaneous affairs. Take into consideration how long healing items take to use – a couple of seconds is a drop in the ocean compared to the length of a match so take time out to heal if it means you're better prepared. This applies at any stage during the match, but particularly worth remembering in the frantic final moments. Those seconds count as extra time to decide your position and how you can approach winning the match.

# KEEP BUILDING

This doesn't mean 'keep practising your builds', you already know that this is an important skill. We mean keep throwing up walls, editing your structures and repairing what you've placed. Most players will keep shooting out your structures, so force them to waste ammo. The more walls you place and the tougher the materials you use, the more ammo enemies will spend to get to you.

# GOODBYE

So, there we have it. We survived the black hole of Chapter 1 and its ending and discovered everything there is to know in the brave new world of Chapter 2.

We've angled for weapons and unusually healthy aquatic fish. We've hidden in dumpsters, checked out every new location, looked at all the changes made and decided which weapons we like best. You've learned new tactics and how to dominate the new island with your squad.

It's a new experience, but underneath, it's the same Fortnite we've learned to love. Equip your favourite skin, show off your new emotes and get ready for more seasons and more changes.

It's time for you to go to battle, armed with everything you've learned here, and get those Victory Royales. Build better, drop smarter and work together.

Remember, Fortnite is a game and there's so much joy to be had through learning and playing. Do your best, keep practising and above all, have fun.

We'll see you on the Battle Bus!

# NOTES

# SAFETY TIPS

## YOUNGER FANS' GUIDE

Spending time online is great fun. As *Fortnite* might be your first experience of digital socialising, here are a few simple rules to help you stay safe and keep the internet an awesome place to spend time:
• Never give out your real name – don't use it as your username.
• Never give out any of your personal details.
• Never tell anybody which school you go to or how old you are.
• Never tell anybody your password, except a parent or guardian.
• Before registering with *Fortnite*, ask a parent or guardian for permission.
• Take regular breaks, as well as playing with parents nearby, or in shared family rooms.
• Always tell a parent or guardian if something is worrying you.

> **NOTE**
> *Fortnite: Battle Royale* is PEGI rated 12

## PARENTS' GUIDE

### ONLINE CHAT

In *Fortnite*, there is live, unmoderated voice and on-screen text chat between users. At the time of writing, turning off text chat isn't possible. You can, however, turn off voice chat:
• Open the Settings menu in the top right of the main *Fortnite* page, then the cog icon. Choose the Audio tab at the top of the screen. From there, you can adjust several audio features, including voice chat. Turn the setting from 'on' to 'off' by tapping the arrows.
• On consoles, you are also able to disable voice chat completely in the Parental Controls, or you can set it so your child can only chat with users who have previously been added as friends. It's important to stress to your child that they shouldn't add anyone as a friend they don't know in real life. To find these controls, see opposite about in-game purchases.

### SOCIAL MEDIA SCAMS

There are many accounts on Facebook and Twitter that claim to give away free V-Bucks, which will be transferred to their account. Be sceptical – it's important to check the authenticity of these accounts and offers before giving away personal information.

### SOUND

*Fortnite* is a game where sound is crucial. Players will often wear headphones, meaning parents won't be able to hear what is being said by strangers. Set up your console or computer to have sound coming from the TV as well as the headset so you can hear what other players are saying to your child.

### REPORTING PLAYERS

If you see or hear a player being abusive, you can easily report them.
• Open the Settings menu in the main *Fortnite* page. Select the Feedback option, which allows you to report bugs, send comments or report players.
• After you've been eliminated from a game, you're also given an option to report a player by holding down the corresponding button at the bottom of the screen.

### SCREEN TIME

Taking regular breaks is important. Set play sessions by using a timer. However, *Fortnite* games can last up to 20 minutes and if your child finishes playing in the middle of a round, they'll leave their teammates a person short and lose any points they've earned. So, it is advisable to give an advanced warning for stopping play.

### IN-GAME PURCHASES

*Fortnite* does offer the ability to make in-game purchases such as new clothes, dances (emotes) and equipment, but they're not required to play the game. They also don't improve a player's performance.

To set up parental controls:
• For PlayStation 4, you can create special child accounts that can be linked to your adult account, which lets you set monthly spending limits. Log into your main PS4 account. Go to Settings > Parental Controls > Family Management. Choose Add Family Member > Create User, and then enter your child's name and date of birth. You can set up specific parental controls.

• For Xbox One, you can create a special passcode to verify purchases. Go to Settings > All Settings > Accounts > Sign-in. Then choose Change My Sign-In & Security Preferences, and scroll right to Customise. Scroll right again and select Ask For My Passkey To Make Purchases, and choose Passkey Required. Simply pick a PIN your child won't guess.

• For PC and Mac, go into the account settings of your child's Epic Games account. Once in there, make sure there aren't any card details or linked PayPal accounts. You can easily remove them if they are there.

• For iPhone and iPad, whenever you make a purchase, you'll always have to verify it with either a password, the Touch ID fingerprint scanner or Face ID. But some iPhones are set up so that you only have to enter a password every 15 minutes. To stop this, go to Settings > Your Name > iTunes & App Store. Underneath you'll see a Password Settings Section. Go to Purchases And In-App Purchases, and choose Always Require. If your child knows your iPhone password, you can set up a second PIN for purchases. Go to Settings > General > Restrictions, then press Enable Restrictions. Choose a new four-digit passcode for In-App Purchases.